THE
WESTMORLAND
LAKES
IN OLD PHOTOGRAPHS

MRS HESKETT was an original member of the Langdale Linen 'Industry' founded by John Ruskin and was left in charge at St Martins, Elterwater when Canon Rawnsley (founder of the National Trust) and his housekeeper Marion Twelves moved to Keswick in 1889.

THE
WESTMORLAND
LAKES

IN OLD PHOTOGRAPHS

COLLECTED BY

JOHN MARSH

ALAN SUTTON

Alan Sutton Publishing Limited
Phoenix Mill · Far Thrupp · Stroud · Gloucestershire

First published 1992

British Library Cataloguing in Publication Data

Marsh, John
Westmorland Lakes in Old Photographs
I. Title
942.78

ISBN 0-7509-0116-0

THIS BOOK IS DEDICATED
to Mrs Abigail Reed, whose family have roots deep in the district and whose
Christianity has helped many in her long life.

Typeset in 9/10 Korinna.
Typesetting and origination by
Alan Sutton Publishing Limited.
Printed in Great Britain by
The Bath Press, Avon.

CONTENTS

AMBLESIDE RUSHBEARING, 1909.

INTRODUCTION

This is the second part of a trilogy covering the rural areas of the old administrative County of Westmorland. *South Westmorland Villages in Old Photographs* was published in 1991, and this volume contains photographs of mid- and north-western Westmorland. It includes a large part of the 'English Lake District', a name superimposed on parts of Westmorland, Cumberland and North Lancashire by the Romantic movement and the holiday trade. Readers will find mention of the Romantics and the holiday trade, as they can hardly be ignored, but generally the book attempts to find the 'real' Westmorland of landowners, farmers, and country and village folk who for generations lived hereabouts.

The first 'guide' to the Lake District was written by a Jesuit priest, Father Thomas West, who thus started a progress which, combined with the Romantic movement among artists and poets, transformed an area noted for the difficulty of its farming and harshness of its life into an arcadian resort. Poets and writers often considered the local farming folk and villagers to be part of the stupid poor, although many of the locals of the eighteenth and nineteenth centuries must have watched with incredulity the goings on as holiday makers and seekers of 'the romantic' invaded their lands. People scrambling on the fells must have caused many a shepherd to scratch his head. Rock climbing must have caused even more surprise: who could wish to climb for fun what the locals had to climb to rescue their cragfast sheep and kill the ever pervasive pests such as foxes? Many a Westmorland breadwinner had lost his life in places to which the visitors took themselves for enjoyment of the experience of being there. 'Tha wants nowt gaing thear,' must have been muttered many times to the intrepid explorers.

Gradually the amazed Westmerians caught on that this was a way of life offering better reward than the hard farming and industrial life they had existed on previously. The provision of horses, carriages, accommodation, guides and many more of the amazingly diverse range of money-making activities that make up the holiday trade became a way of life. Even the farmers started taking in 'bed and breakfasts'. The Furness and the North Western railway companies formalized, with large capital investment, the holiday trades which have been continued by others to this day. The weather that Westmorland farmers had learned to live with over centuries became an object of humour or was idolized into the romantic. The long winter blizzard that at one time completely wiped out a local farmer's stock, with dire results for him and his family, became something to enjoy as the snow transformed the fells into a 'winter resort'.

Beneath the superficial Romantic and holiday scene the Westmerians continued much as before. The holiday 'season' was significant, but the farming seasons remained more important for many, and the fox a bigger problem than the motor car. This collection of photographs attempts to catch the 'real' scene of a period between fifty and one hundred years ago in an area that contains so much now that is false. It is disconcerting to a local person such as myself to realize that in the last fifty years so much of Westmerian life has been 'planned' out of existence by committees of various sorts on which very little 'real' local representation is to be found. Who, the locals ask, planned the dead villages with no shop, no school, an empty church and houses used as 'holiday homes'? Who 'planned' the drowned village of Mardale? Who planned the ugly 'big shed' estates of industrial building now being attached to almost every settlement.

The area covered fits between the area of the South Westmorland Villages book and the forthcoming Eden Valley volume. It is an area of hills and valleys bounded in the east by the Lune Valley and the Shap Fells and the west by the old counties of Cumberland and that part of Lancashire North of the Sands that was covered in a separate book published in 1991 with my friend John Garbutt as co-author. Wherever possible, the photographer is named against his picture as it was his skills that have left local historians with these important sources of information.

The history of the area may be traced back almost as far as the ice ages which moulded the hills and valleys. One of the country's most ancient industries can be discerned in the axe factories of the Langdale area where ancient man hewed his tools and weapons out of the fells to trade all over Europe. Thick layers of peat cover traces of the hunter-gatherers who worked the forests that once covered this land. The first men to take up residence cut down the forests for fuel and building materials and the livestock they introduced have grazed the land bare ever since. The Romans took the area in their stride, putting roads across the fells and forts in the valleys. The Hiberno-Norse found the district much to their liking and left us their place names and their language in the local dialect which was to last over a thousand years – until today, when it is being killed off by modern English and its social affections. The early Christians found the wilderness suited them and a number of early Christian saints knew the area well. The Normans could make little of it in the first instance but gradually absorbed the lands into their estates, the Barony of Kendale taking some land but leaving the pre-Norman Curwen and Lowther families very much as they were, 'owning' large tracts of land that were not much use for anything except grazing sheep. This fact, along with the monastic estates, gave rise to the medieval wool trade, which brought a sort of prosperity to some in the district. The monastic interests at Shap Abbey and Furness Abbey led to many arguments about boundaries which were only finally resolved when the monasteries were dissolved and their lands handed over to those Tudor land-owners who supported the king.

The seventeenth century was a gloomy time generally, but it produced the estate houses, so much admired by visitors today, when the large estates were divided into tenanted farms. This type of farming was difficult in the extreme, and failure was commonplace and 'weather' a serious subject. Solace was found in religion and many a village church was rebuilt. The nonconformist religions fulfilled many requirements lost to the ordinary folk since the Reformation and suited their tough individuality. In the Lake District area groups of wealthy outsiders bought estates and superimposed themselves on the local scene of landlords and tenants, many adding to the patronage of the Westmerians by the provision of new churches and schools. Some, such as Ruskin, Rawnsley, Ransome and Beatrix Potter, brought with them fame that the tourist industry was able to expoit. The railways arrived in the early nineteenth century and upset the local poet William Wordsworth. The first holiday homes appeared, and by the end of the century the villages of Windermere and Bowness-on-Windermere, undergoing much new building, were lit by electricity, amazingly, the second places in the country to be so illuminated.

This is the time and place covered by this book – steam railways, horse coaches, poor roads – Westmorland in the Lake District, but including an area to the east hardly ever visited by the holiday-maker.

The generosity I discovered among Westmerians before and following the publication of the South Westmorland Villages book has been carried over into this publication in the shape of many pictures and much information that was freely provided and which have enriched the contents in many ways. This book is too small to use all the material provided but I do hope the families concerned are pleased with my use of their private material.

John Marsh
Spring 1992

SECTION ONE

The Kendal Fringe, the Lune, and Shap Fells

THE JAW BONES were a landmark on the road from Kendal to Windermere. It is said that a member of the Bateman family, from nearby Tolson Hall, was a whaling captain who presented the bones to grace the family estate. The photograph of about 1905 was taken by J. Anderson of Kendal.

BURNESIDE HALL viewed through the gatehouse, by Atkinson and Pollitt of Kendal in the 1930s. This ancient hall was once home of the Bellingham and the Braithwaite families but has long been only a farmhouse.

FIRST PRIZE IN THE CLASS AT KENDAL SHOW in 1908 went to John Dargue, Burneside Hall for his Blackfaced Scotch ram. For many years the family took prizes for their breed of Scotch Blackfaced sheep, a breed said to be the original breed of heath sheep from the Middle Ages.

THE ANGLERS INN, BURNESIDE about 1905 when Mrs Mary Preston was the licensee. The neighbours have turned out to be included in the photograph.

CROPPER'S BURNESIDE PAPER MILL in 1904. This mill has been manufacturing paper since 1833, the Cropper family acquiring the business in 1845.

BURNESIDE POST OFFICE about 1905 when John Cunningham was postmaster. Letters arrived 6.30 a.m. and 3.20 p.m. and were despatched 11.20 a.m., 6.05 p.m. and 9.13 p.m. Sunday night despatch was at 6 p.m. with Sunday opening for stamps and telegrams from 8 a.m. to 10 a.m.

HAYMAKING in the field next to Burneside station about 1905. This was hard, back-breaking work, with all the members of the family joining in.

BURNESIDE STATION about 1902, by Ewan of Kendal. The London and North Western line was opened through Burneside to Windermere in 1847 only two years after James Cropper had acquired the paper mill. The station and railway activities at Burneside were very much influenced by the mill.

THE INSTITUTE AND HOLM LYNN, BURNESIDE, again by Ewan of Kendal. The Bryce Institute, built in 1897 with money provided by John Bryce, a manager of Cropper's Mill, had not long been opened when the photograph was taken. The building provided recreational and educational facilities for the workpeople of Burneside, and even bathing facilities for a time.

REFLECTIONS in the mill dam at Cowan Head about 1905, by Ewan of Kendal. The mill at Cowan Head dates back to 1750 when it was run by Mr T. Ashburner of Kendal and, like Burneside Mill, was acquired by the Cropper family in 1845.

DODDING GREEN, SKELSMERGH in 1892. Skelsmergh was home to many who followed the 'old religion' after the Reformation, and it was where Thomas Sprott was born in 1576. He became a priest and was executed at Lincoln in 1600 in the frenzy of unchristian activity of those days. The Stephensons of Whinfell, Bannisdale and Dodding Green was another such family. A church was endowed at Dodding Green in 1716 and the house left to the Catholic church on Robert Stephenson's death.

WILLIAM RICHARDSON OF LAVEROCK BRIDGE took first prize in the class for a 'half-bred shearling gimmer' with his Wensleydale/Rough Fell ewe at Kendal show in September 1909.

MR AND MRS WILLIAM WOOF of Clawthorpe Hall, Burton-in-Kendal went for a ride on their motor cycle combination in 1913 and were photographed in passing at Laverock Bridge. Leather leggings and clogs were appropriate wear but how did the hats stop on?

MEALBANK MILL photographed by J. Sawyers of Kendal about 1905. Braithwaite and Co. established their woollen mill, and this was joined by Samuel Gawith's Snuff Mill. Braithwaites erected a 'commodious school in which is a reading room and library' in 1868. The school building was also used as the local Methodist chapel.

SCARFOOT COTTAGES, MEALBANK photographed by Ewan of Kendal about 1905. Mealbank is in the parish of Scalthwaiterigg (which is old Norse for a hut in a clearing on the ridge). Much of it was the land of the Leper Hospital of St Leonard (now Spital Farm) until the Reformation.

THE MEALBANK ASSOCIATION FOOTBALL CLUB in the last season before the First World War. The players are joined by eight officials for the team photograph. Players that year included Craghill, Long, Willcock, Hine, Reed, Scholfield and Robinson. The very local game against Burneside Old Boys on 21 September 1913 produced the happy result of a 2–2 draw.

GATE HOUSE SHOP, SCALTHWAITERIGG about 1905 when Miss Mary Agnes Graham was the shopkeeper. Her neighbours were Arthur Bell and John Graham and their families. Mr Bell and Mr Graham worked as railway signalmen on the adjoining London and North Western Railway.

THORNLEIGH, SKELSMERGH when Thomas Storey, 'Builder and Contractor', lived there. The postcard, dated 2 November 1903, is from Ruth Storey to her friend Miss Roberta Robinson at Rock Cottage, Newby Bridge and says, 'This is my home and my mother is in the garden.'

MOUNT QUHARRIE, SKELSMERGH just before the First World War. William Wilberforce Thwaites lived here in 1910 and a Mrs Dugdale is recorded in 1913 at about the time of the picture.

GRAYRIGG RAILWAY STATION on the London and North Western Railway about 1910, with station master, porter and three passengers for the 'Down' train to the north. This station closed in 1954 and the site has been cleared.

THE GRAYRIGG SMITHY about 1905, by J. Sawyers of Kendal, when Thomas Park of Chapel Houses was the farrier. Through the late nineteenth century John William Croft was the blacksmith.

THE ALMSHOUSES AT GRAYRIGG photographed in about 1905 by J. Anderson of Kendal. The six almshouses were erected and endowed in 1868 by Miss Mary Rowlandson of Akay Lodge, Sedbergh and her brothers 'for the aged and indigent'.

THE NORTH END OF GRAYRIGG VILLAGE about 1905, showing Dale House and the adjoining cottages with a barn where the post office is now situated, photographed by J. Sawyers of Kendal. In 1905 the post office was at Chapel Houses, with Miss M.A. Langhorn as postmistress. 'Letters arrive 7 a.m. and are despatched 4.15 p.m', says a guide of the period.

THE PLOUGHING COMPETITION held at Grayrigg Hall farm about 1905. The ploughing matches were started in 1810 by the Kendal Agricultural Society and soon became part of the farming year. The Selside, Grayrigg and Mountain District Agricultural Society (founded in 1857 out of the High Borrow Bridge Cattle Show) held alternate ploughings at Selside Hall and Grayrigg Hall.

THE FRIENDS MEETING HOUSE at Beckfoot, Beckhouses, near Grayrigg about 1907. In his book, *The Quaker Meeting Houses of the Lake Counties* (1978), David Butler tells how this 'meeting' originated in 1696 and the building was enlarged in 1713. By 1846 the building was disused but there was a second occupation with complete rebuild in 1871 – this included a cottage. The meeting house seen here was closed in 1952 and the building sold.

LILYMERE photographed by Jackson and Sons for Sedbergh School about 1910. This picture then appeared in the school series of postcards to advertise the school and to send home to parents. An ancient lake in the parish of Killington, Lilymere could be fished for char, a fish which is commonly found in Windermere and is said to pre-date the Ice Age.

ST JOHN'S CHURCH, FIRBANK at the turn of the century. This marks the extreme eastern boundary of this book's coverage. Across the nearby River Lune was Yorkshire. The church was built in 1842 after the previous church, built in 1742, blew down in a gale in the winter of 1839/40.

THE LOWGILL AREA near Beckfoot. The first view is looking towards the Lowgill Viaduct on the Lowgill to Ingleton railway line about 1930, photographed by Atkinson and Pollitt of Kendal. This railway line was opened in 1861 and finally closed in 1965. The second picture shows Beckfoot, Lowgill, photographed by J. Simcoe and Son of Kendal about 1910.

INTO THE TEBAY VALLEY from the road to Grayrigg in the late 1920s by Atkinson and Pollitt – Harold Simcoe was probably the photographer. Note the motorcycle registration number EC2800.

WHINFELL PRIMITIVE METHODIST SALE OF WORK was visited at the turn of the century by photographer Ashworth of Kendal, who pictured the minister and a number of the flock attending. The Primitives were an 1810 schism from the Methodist Church which was not repaired until the reunion of 1932. In his book on the history of local Methodism (Kendal, 1987), Percy Bryer relates that there were five societies on the Kendal Primitive circuit, of which Whinfell was one, with nineteen members in 1893.

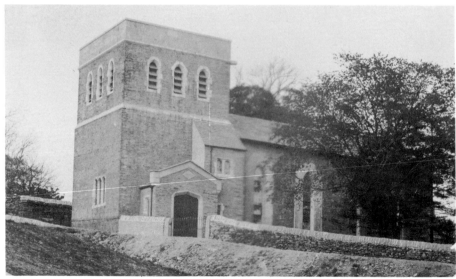

ST THOMAS'S CHURCH, SELSIDE WITH WHITWELL stands among fields in a scattered community of about 300 people. Built on this site in 1838, it was restored in 1894. The photograph dates from about 1905 and was used on a postcard to Miss D. Phillipson at Bowston, asking Dora to ask 'Cissey to call at Miss Kooks, I will send a parcel thir for her.'

SELSIDE CHURCH INTERIOR about 1905, with a fine collection of oil lamps. The site of the original eighteenth-century church is a number of yards away from the 1838 church, and it is said that William Thornburgh of Selside Hall, one of the local ancient families who had not changed their ways at the Reformation, obtained permission to change the chapel at the Hall to Catholic use so long as he gave the land for the building of a church nearby.

SELSIDE VICARAGE about 1905 when the Revd Joseph J. Clarke was the vicar. At that time Anthony Atkinson of Selside Hall was the chairman of the parish meeting, James Dixon of Kitt Cragg was Rural District councillor, Thomas Walker of East Above Park clerk of the School Endowment Fund, and Henry Jennings of Long Well secretary of the Selside and Grayrigg Agricultural Society.

CHAPLOW OF HELSINGTON'S THRASHING MACHINE at Selside Hall before the First World War, when Mr W. Parkin was the tenant farmer. Besides Mr and Mrs Parkin, on the picture are members of the Knowles, Sutton, Jennings, Ridding and Walker families.

SHAW END, PATTON about 1905. This postcard was used by the owner, Arthur Shaw, as a New Year's greeting in 1906 to Miss Martindale of Meadow Bank, Didsbury: 'Best wishes for 1906 – when are you coming this way?'

THE PLOUGH INN AT SELSIDE, seen here in the 1920s, took its name from an establishment on a very old coach road still traceable in fields at the rear. The barn door signed 'Garage' is an indication of the changes taking place. A century earlier, in 1822, the Heron Syke to Eamont Bridge Turnpike Trust started their new road over Shap Fell, the first section being in Selside. Photo by J. Simcoe.

FIVE MEMBERS OF THE SAME FAMILY WERE KILLED when a German bomber unloaded his bombs on Selside in April 1941. The Wood family had been at Cooper (or Cowper) House for many years before the disaster took place. A total of eleven people, including five adults evacuated there, were killed and two injured. The *Westmorland Gazette* of 26 April 1941, using restricted wartime reporting, could not use the name of the farm and said 'a farmhouse in the north-west of England'.

SELSIDE SCHOOLCHILDREN *en route* to school before the First World War, photographed by Platt of Kendal. Robert Kitching of Borrowdale Head was contracted by Westmorland County Council to use a 'large float with a movable cover' to convey the Fawcett Forest children to school but was caught on this day overloading his farm spring cart. The photograph was taken at the end of the lane from the A6 to the school.

THE BLACKSMITH'S SHOP AND POST OFFICE at Watchgate, Selside just after the First World War, photographed by J. Simcoe of Kendal. The main A6 road shows nothing of the traffic problems about to take place. This was the home of the Tallon family, who had the post office and smithy for over sixty years, following a tradition set up by William Rack who was also a combined blacksmith and postmaster.

RUTH AND LENORE HUCK AT HOLLOWGATE FARM, Selside in December 1937. It was considered a 'bad enough' winter, but worse was to come – see p. 35. This photograph was supplied by Mrs Lenore Knowles (née Huck) of Hollowgate, who looked after the famous roadside 'Leyland Clock' nearby until the opening of the M6 motorway rendered it obsolete.

THE FIRST SUMMIT on the A6 road over Shap Fell was near Gateside Farm at the 'Leyland Clock'. The view south from near that point is here photographed in the 1920s by Atkinson and Pollitt of Kendal. Hollowgate is the farm in the centre of the picture. The continuation of the A6 over Shap, including 'Huck's Brow' which took its name from Mrs Knowles' family, will be found in *The Eden Valley in Old Photographs*.

THE 'LEYLAND CLOCK' in the blizzard of February/March 1941, in another of Mrs Knowles' photographs showing lorries trapped by the snow which closed the road for six days in 'the worst snow for fifty years'. The Patterdale hunt pack had been visiting Longsleddale and was trapped there for thirteen days.

THE UNMADE ROAD leading from the A6 to Garnett Bridge in the 1920s, with the usual traces of horse traffic, photographed by Atkinson and Pollitt of Kendal.

GARNETT BRIDGE, in the parish of Strickland Roger, about 1905 when the hamlet had two mills driven by water power from the River Sprint – a sawmill and a bobbin mill.

LONGSLEDDALE CHURCH AND SCHOOL, together with the parsonage, were rebuilt in 1863 by Mrs Howard of Levens Hall who was 'lady of the manor' at the time. The first picture, by Ewan of Kendal in about 1905, shows the photographer's trap parked in the lane near the school. The second picture is of the same period and shows the interior of the church with the lighting by oil lamp.

A SUMMER'S DAY IN LONGSLEDDALE about 1910. Mary Taylor used this postcard in July 1913 to tell her sister at Mint Cottage, 'I will be out on Tuesday.'

FISHWICKS FARM IN LONGSLEDDALE photographed about 1910 by Simcoe and Son of Kendal. Sixteen people had assembled in front of the farm to watch the goings on, while three boys have wandered closer to watch the photographer.

LONGSLEDDALE AT DALE END photographed by J. Sawyers of Kendal about 1905 when Henry Dowthwaite lived there – is it Henry in the road? Tenter How, a name harking back to the medieval wool trade, is in the background. John Robinson had the farm in those days.

CROOK OLD CHURCH TOWER about 1905. This ancient site was abandoned, leaving only the tower standing, in 1887 when St Catherine's church was built by the roadside a few hundred yards away.

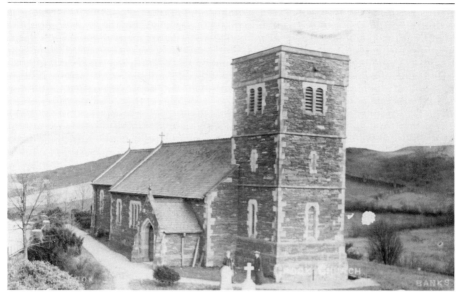

ST CATHERINE'S CHURCH, CROOK at the turn of the century, photographed by Banks of Kendal. That Crook had a church in the Middle Ages is confirmed by the very ancient bell preserved from previous churches and now in the 'new' church.

CROOK about 1910. The Eller Beck had for centuries powered a number of mills in the parish; Crook was described as a 'hive of industry with three mills'. The Crook Mill was joined by the Sever Mill, the Birch Mill and (just in the adjoining parish) the Ellerbank Mill. At various times over the years these were used for corn milling, bobbin making, bone grinding, engineering, and even to power the house at Ellerbank with electricity.

THE WILD BOAR HOTEL, CROOK. In the first photograph (from the early 1930s, by Atkinson and Pollitt of Kendal) an exterior much changed from today can be seen, and in the second the interior entrance hall is caught about 1920 by Herbert and Sons of Windermere.

THE WOODYARD AT STAVELEY BOBBIN MILL about 1905, showing the cart used to bring the wood into the yard. The Staveley Wood Turning Company business has survived although bobbin turning has been discontinued. James B. Woodward, who lived at Mill House, was the manager when the picture was taken.

FELLFOOT COTTAGES AT STAVELEY photographed by Ewan of Kendal about 1902 when the Hebson family, James Phillipson (a carter), and William Bewsher (who sold refreshments) lived there.

STAVELEY LEVEL CROSSING over the Oxenholme to Windermere railway lines about 1904, pictured by Ashworths of Kendal. Traffic along the main road was often interrupted by the closure of these gates by the level crossing keeper who lived in the nearby cottage. William Watson is listed as crossing keeper when this photograph was taken.

JOHN FAULKNER'S 'CASH' GROCERY SHOP in the centre of Staveley village about 1910, by J. Simcoe of Kendal. In the background can be seen the Abbey Home for orphans run by the Kendal Guardians of the Poor Law Union. This fine mansion had previously been the home of the Johnson family.

ON THE KENTMERE ROAD out of Staveley village about 1903, with Anthony Swidenbank's tailors and drapery shop on the left, and on the right the side windows and chimney of Threlfall's grocery shop.

STAVELEY MAIN STREET about 1907, photographed by J. Simcoe of Kendal, shows the Kendal Bank and, just beyond, the Fat Lamb beerhouse when George Cannon had the licence. The Fat Lamb was closed in October 1913.

STATION ROAD, STAVELEY about 1905, with a long heap of roadmaking stones lining one side of the road. The inhabitants of the road at the time included William Parrington, the station master, Henry Storey, the builder, S.J. Parrington, the beerhouse keeper at the Railway Tavern, John Alfred Turner, a platelayer on the railway, and Dick Mitchell Innes MB, ChB, medical officer and 'factory surgeon' at Stanley Bank.

STAVELEY RAILWAY STATION about 1905 when William Parrington was the station master for the London and North Western Railway Company. Staveley has been an unmanned halt since 1971. In 1973 one of the tracks was removed.

ST JAMES'S CHURCH, STAVELEY about 1905 when the Revd William Chaplin was vicar. Built in 1865 to designs by J.S. Crowther and much restored in 1887, these three lancet windows contain important examples of Victorian stained glass by Burne-Jones from the factory of Morris & Co.

THE TOWER of the St Margaret's 'old' church at Staveley dates back to the fifteenth century. In spite of much rebuilding the old church site was most unsatisfactory and a new church was built in 1865 leaving the old tower to grace the main street. This became a clock tower from 1887 when W.B. Thornton presented a clock to celebrate the Queen's Jubilee. Photo by H. Blakey of Staveley.

THE STAVELEY SCHOOL BAZAAR of October 1927 was a three day event in aid of the school buildings. It was organized to help finance a new classroom, boiler house, furnace and water supply as well as new internal partitions and cloak room. It coincided with one of the worst storms for many years. The *Westmorland Gazette* of 5 November 1927 had two pages of the disasters over the previous weekend. Lady Henry Cavendish-Bentinck from Underley opened the event with Mr J.W. Cropper presiding. The first picture shows the car park with the marquee firmly in place on 29 October, and the second the unfortunate results of the gale. Many who attended had difficulty getting home.

A VIEW INSIDE THE SCHOOL for the 1927 bazaar, showing the local guide troop with their sweet and gift stall. A history of the school was on sale but there were complaints that hardly any mention was made of Mr Herbert Anderton, the late headmaster, who had served the school for twenty-two years.

SCROGGS FARM, STAVELEY on 2 November 1904 when J. and T. Brocklebank were the farmers.

KENTMERE CHURCH OF ST CUTHBERT photographed about 1902 by Sawyers of Kendal. In the background is Kentmere Hall (see p. 53) and the Garburn pass to Troutbeck. A restoration of the very ancient fabric in 1866 added the tower paid for by Admiral Wilson of The Howe, Windermere. It is said that this is one of the most ancient of the Christian sites in the district.

THE INTERIOR OF KENTMERE CHURCH about 1905 shows the stove, sited to provide warmth to the choir and the parson, and no lighting. The barn-like interior of this most ancient of local churches is very obvious in this picture.

KENTMERE HALL dates back to the fourteenth century and is famous locally as the home of the Gilpin family whose traditions include the killing of the last boar (which then became part of their heraldry) and for Barnard Gilpin, 'the apostle of the north', whose life spanned the Reformation and who, since he went into the church after being at Oxford University, had great difficulty in surviving the unchristian activities of that time. The photograph is of about 1905 when William Gregg was the farmer.

RESTON COTTAGES, STAVELEY about 1914 when the main road was at the front door.

RESTON, STAVELEY by Sawyer of Kendal about 1905 when the house was the residence of Mr T.W. and Mr J.L. Johnson who are both likely to be seen on the picture.

ST ANNE'S CHURCH, INGS about 1905 by Sawyer of Kendal. Situated on the site of a much earlier church in Hugill parish, this classical church built in 1743 by Robert Bateman, who had originated at Reston Hall, had a major restoration in 1878.

THE INTERIOR OF ST ANNE'S, INGS in the late 1920s, by Atkinson and Pollitt of Kendal, shows the lighting was still by oil lamp.

Meadowcroft Hotel, Ings.

LOOKING DOWN ON MEADOWCROFT, INGS in the 1930s when the main road still curved through by the church. The petrol pumps on the left were the beginning of a major change for this corner of the parish. The photograph is by Atkinson and Pollitt of Kendal.

Bowness, Windermere and Troutbeck

SAILING A WINDERMERE YACHT about 1912 in a photograph by G.P. Abraham of Keswick. It is reported that these yachts, with their heavy keels to counterbalance the mast and sails, sank 'like a stone' under certain circumstances.

STORRS HALL was built by Sir John Legard in 1790 and much altered in 1807 when John Bolton was the owner. The architect then was J.M. Gandy of Liverpool who had just constructed the Storrs Temple of Heroes nearby. The house became the Grand Hotel at the turn of the century, and is here seen in the 1920s when the name Storrs Hall was again in use. Photo by Atkinson and Pollitt of Kendal.

BELSFIELD was built to Websters of Kendal design in 1844. It was the home of industrialist Henry Schneider from 1869 to 1887 when it became a hotel. Photographer Brockbank of Windermere caught a Riggs coach at the door in about 1910.

SIR HENRY SEAGRAVE was within seconds of disaster when Atkinson and Pollitt photographed *Miss England II* travelling at a speed of 119 m.p.h. on Friday 13 June 1930. Sir Henry and mechanic Vic Halliwell died, but mechanic Michael Willcocks survived, when the boat flipped over.

SKATING ON WINDERMERE, 2 March 1929, was one of a series of postcards issued by Atkinson and Pollitt of Kendal during that hard winter when a late frost took everyone by surprise. Motor cars were driven on the lake's frozen surface and the hotels reopened for the visitors taking advantage of the winter sports.

BOWNESS BAY, WINDERMERE in the late nineteenth century, with the steam yacht *Esperance*, which was then used as a ferry by the Ferry Hotel, waiting for guests at the pier. This yacht was originally a private steam yacht built in 1869 for Henry Schneider of Belsfield, and was later acquired by the Ferry Hotel to carry their guests across the lake. She still survives and can be seen at the Windermere Steamboat Museum. She also appeared in the film *Swallows and Amazons* as Captain Flint's houseboat.

THE BOWNESS-ON-WINDERMERE SEA SCOUTS at camp about 1914 with their leader Mr Sladen. This troop had been founded in 1912, based on a scout troop only four years older, by John Mortimer Sladen of Cleeve Howe, Windermere, a close friend of Sir Robert Baden-Powell, the originator of the Boy Scout movement.

ON BOARD THE BEAVER awaiting the arrival of Major General Sir Robert Baden-Powell on 29 August 1915 when Sir Robert and Lady Baden-Powell were taken to Fell Foot after visiting scouts in the Windermere area. Scouting in the Windermere area received a further boost in May 1936 when W.B. Wakefield, brother of E.W. Wakefield of Kendal, gave Great Tower plantation, just over the border in Lancashire, to the movement.

THE STEAM YACHT *BRITANNIA* was built in 1879 for Colonel Ridehalgh of Fell Foot. She was sold in 1907 to the Furness Railway and was used originally as a directors' yacht but then let for party hire. She is seen here at Bowness pier about 1910. *Britannia* was scrapped in 1919 having been taken out of service in 1915.

RIGG'S COACH at Ferry Nab about 1914. The Rigg's coach service to Coniston was a popular trip as it included a journey on the ferry across Windermere.

THE ULLSWATER COACH pulling away from Bowness, passing St Martin's church, about 1910. This was another popular trip run by Riggs and included the climb over the infamous Kirkstone Pass – see p. 148 – the scene of many accidents which were reported in the local press.

THE ROYAL SQUARE, BOWNESS decorated for the Jubilee of Queen Victoria in 1887. The celebratory parade took place on a 'hot sunny day'.

QUEENS SQUARE, BOWNESS-ON-WINDERMERE, by Stengal & Co. about 1907, showing a hotel 'bus' passing the Royal Hotel.

TWO VIEWS OF THE FERRY from Ferry Nab, Bowness, Westmorland to Claife in High Furness, Lancashire. The first, by Brunskill and Sons, shows the row-boat ferry which was replaced by a steam ferry in 1870. In the second view the first steam ferry, complete with lifeboat and anchor, can be seen with a load of full coaches.

THE ORIGINAL STEAM FERRY in its last years. There are two guide ropes for safety and the Ferry Hotel bus is on board. In the second picture, of the early 1920s, Atkinson and Pollitt of Kendal have pictured the boat which replaced the original steam ferry in 1915. The vehicles then carried had become motorized.

BOWNESS-ON-WINDERMERE JUNIOR SCHOOL CHILDREN, with teacher Miss Nichol, pose for the class photograph in about 1925. The twins on the second row are Eric and Clifford Dixon, with Leslie Moss and Renie Morton to the left. This picture has been supplied by the Moss family of Windermere.

WINDERMERE, 19 August 1919, victory celebrations. Second prize-winner for a decorated perambulator was Mrs Annie Burton, seen with her daughter May. Annie originated from The Bield, Little Langdale. In the second picture one of Rigg's coaches can be seen passing Herbert and Sons photographic studio opposite St Martin's church in the parade which preceded the Dawes meadow event. Windermere fire engine was voted the 'best decorated' in the parade.

ST MARTIN'S CHURCH, BOWNESS, photographed by Brunskill and Son of Windermere in 1869 before the extensive alterations of 1870–3. This view was reproduced onto postcards at the turn of the century.

MAIN STREET, BOWNESS at the turn of the century. The cottages on the left were demolished before the First World War as part of a road improvement scheme.

THE ROYAL HOTEL with the Riggs coaches for Coniston and Ullswater standing back to back awaiting their passengers in a Stengal picture of about 1902. Note the ornamental balconies which originally graced this hotel.

THE CHESTNUT TREE, CRAGG BROW, Bowness-on-Windermere, with Frank 'Fenty' Robinson's 'other' shop, on a postcard issued in May 1906 with an appeal to save the tree. The appeal included a verse, part of which is: 'The first to blossom, the last to fade/In vernal loveliness once more arrayed.'

LAKE ROAD, BOWNESS-ON-WINDERMERE about 1905. Biskey Howe Road is on the left, with one of the electric street lights which illuminated the Windermere area by night. The power was supplied by the Windermere and District Electric Company's hydro-electric plant at Troutbeck Bridge.

ST HERBERT'S ROMAN CATHOLIC CHURCH at Windermere was built in Princes Road in 1884 with Robert Walker as architect. In the first picture, by Brunskill and Son, the church can be seen just after completion. The lower picture shows the interior of the church during the period of major problems when the building appeared almost ready to fall down. As the problems became impossible to remedy a new church was planned and opened in 1962 and this site became a tennis court.

MAIN ROAD, WINDERMERE in about 1902, with John Mudd's fishmongers shop, on a postcard sent to Master Gilbert Dugdale of Hendon, London by Jack Middleton of 13 Alexander Road, Bowness which says, 'You will see me on the cart in front of the shop.'

PRIZE-WINNER at Windermere poultry show about 1920 was Walter Burton of Greenriggs, Upper Oak Street. It is said that Walter took his hens into his cellar for a shampoo before he entered them into the show. See other prize-winners in this family on p. 69.

WINDERMERE RAILWAY STATION about 1902. The first view shows the interior of the station on platform 2 when it was a busy terminus of the London and North Western Railway's branch line from Oxenholme. This site is now the interior of a supermarket. On the second picture, by Brockbank and Son, the exterior can be seen, with hotel buses pulling out of the station yard and passing the drinking fountain which is now in the garden of the Brewery Arts Centre in Kendal.

THE RIGG'S COACH FOR KESWICK in the station yard at Windermere railway station. This was the centre of much of the Rigg enterprise, Richard Rigg running the Windermere Hotel and John Rigg the Mail and Coach Office at the station. The route to Keswick from Windermere station was one of the last Royal Mail horse coach routes in the country.

WINDERMERE STATION YARD with an early motor charabanc. Note the primitive radiator arrangement – an attempt to stop overheating on the many hills in the area. A Rigg's coachman sits on the bank seat in the firm's uniform top hat – was he musing on the future or saying, as many did, 'They can't last?'

THE RIGG'S KESWICK COACH outside Rigg's Windermere Hotel about 1905. The Rigg family originated at Middleton near Kirkby Lonsdale and were made wealthy by the holiday coach and hotel business which they entered in the early nineteenth century as the railways expanded the holiday trade.

THE WINDERMERE RESERVOIR on 6 October 1913, photographed by Brockbank of Windermere. The *Westmorland Gazette* of 11 October carried an article on the 'Scarcity of Water' and reported that since 24 September the area's supply was turned off 'except from breakfast time to 1 p.m.' The reservoir water level had dropped from a low of 16 ft 6 in to 5 ft 3 in in a week. The Windermere Gas and Water Company manager, Mr J. Duxbury, is reported to have wished he had the power to 'smite the rock as Moses had done'.

BOYS OF THE OLD COLLEGE, WINDERMERE pose on a felled tree in the grounds of the school with the logging horses in the background in about 1920.

FORM TWO BOYS gather at the greenhouse for a class picture in December 1907.

TROUTBECK BRIDGE WITH MOTOR TRAFFIC pictured by J. Simcoe and Son of Kendal about 1920. Note the Cottage Linen Industry on the left. The postcard sent to Liverpool says, 'Having a fine time here. We have shocked all the natives jazzing in the village hall and making eyes at all the boys. Some life. Love Edie.'

THE COTTAGE LINEN INDUSTRY at Troutbeck Bridge advertises Greek lace and Art needlework at the Troutbeck Bridge post office. This business was founded here by the Misses Dick as a branch of the Cottage Home Industries founded by John Ruskin in Langdale in the nineteenth century which gave 'welcome occupation and assistance to many homes' until foreign products undercut prices after the First World War. Troutbeck Bridge and the Spinnery, Bowness continued long after many had given up.

AT CALGARTH Lord Kerry, son of the Marquis of Lansdowne and the Conservative parliamentary candidate for North Westmorland in the 1906 election, visits Major Noble, the 1905 contender. Major Noble had lost to Mr Lief Jones, the Liberal candidate in the March by-election and Lord Kerry also lost, again to Mr Lief Jones, by *three* votes in the 24 January 1906 election.

CALGARTH PARK from the garden side about 1904. The postcard from Edith at Calgarth asks Miss Sarah Vickers at Hammerbank, 'If it is convenient will you come and have tea with me on Sunday.'

CALGARTH PARK became a hospital for wounded soldiers during the First World War. Much local effort went into helping the unfortunate soldiers. Here the Windermere sea scouts take a bathchair bound soldier for an outing.

THE CAMP CALGARTH · WINDERMERE

BEFORE THE WAR Calgarth Park had been the scene of a number of Volunteer Camps. This shows the 1905 camp where the soldiers trained for the horrors to come.

TROUTBECK POST OFFICE in the 1920s, when Thomas Brown was sub-postmaster, by Matthews of Bradford. Guides advised that 'the nearest Money Order Office' was at Troutbeck Bridge and that Windermere was the 'nearest Telegraph Office', although 'telegrams can be sent by the telephone at the Institute.'

LOW FOLD FARM, TROUTBECK in the 1920s pictured by Matthews of Bradford when Aaron Sisson was listed as farmer 'and apartments'. The bed and breakfast trade would have supplemented his farming income.

SHEEP IN ROBIN LANE, TROUTBECK about 1914. Troutbeck has a division of three 'hundreds', each of which had a bull, a constable and a bridge at the turn of the century, giving the locals the boast that Troutbeck had three hundred bulls, three hundred constables and three hundred bridges.

THE VILLAGE SHOP AT TROUTBECK pictured by Grace Castree of Troutbeck about 1905, Grace Castree published many pictures of Troutbeck about this time.

JESUS CHURCH, TROUTBECK at the turn of the century. This church was rebuilt in 1763 and altered in 1861. In 1897 a clock, paid for by public subscription, was put in the tower. Note the heap of roadstone for filling potholes in the unmade road.

THE BROWNE'S HOUSE AT TROUTBECK is now owned by the National Trust, but in this picture of about 1902 it was still occupied, with a working farm adjoining, by George Browne at Townend House and George Walker at the farm.

WALKING FROM TROUTBECK TO KIRKSTONE PASS in the 1920s, photographed by Atkinson and Pollitt of Kendal.

MARGARET LONGMIRE OF TROUTBECK photographed on 15 April 1864 by J. Garnett of Windermere post office 'on the 100th anniversary of her birthday'. The *Westmorland Gazette* of the time reported her to be 'in good health and in possession of all her faculties'. Her grandson, Thomas Longmire, became a famous Cumberland and Westmorland style wrestler.

TROUTBECK CONGREGATIONAL CHURCH INTERIOR about 1910 at the harvest festival – even the lights were hung with garlands.

THE SUN HOTEL AT TROUTBECK BRIDGE in the 1930s by Atkinson and Pollitt. Note the electric street light and the tree which was missed by the road widening and which protruded into the road by the hotel for many decades.

THE LOW WOOD HOTEL, (above) as seen from the steamer pier in the 1920s by J. Simcoe of Kendal, and (below) with the Rigg's Royal Mail coach for Keswick at the door in about 1905. This hotel was greatly expanded in 1859 by the Logan family, John Logan, who died in 1909, having married the eldest daughter of Richard Rigg of the Windermere Hotel. Mrs Logan's brother ran the Windermere Hotel after their father.

THE STEAMER *SWIFT* sailing into the next part of the book at Ambleside from the Low Wood pier in the early 1920s. The *Swift* was built in 1900 for the Furness Railway Company and is still on the lake. The photograph is by Atkinson and Pollitt of Kendal.

Ambleside, Langdale and Grasmere

THE *SWIFT* arrives at Ambleside pier in this Raphael Tuck photograph taken for the Furness Railway about 1910. Tucks were commissioned to produce sets of postcards for the Furness Railway during the years 1909–12 and these, of course, included the lake steamers.

AMBLESIDE STEAMER PIER about 1904, again by Raphael Tuck but this time in their earlier 'Town and Country' series. Hotel buses wait while the original *Swan* (1869–1938) unloads her passengers.

WATERHEAD, AMBLESIDE was visited by Payne Jennings in the 1870s. The boatyard and roadside barn stand beside the small 1840 Waterhead Hotel. The scene is much changed today.

THE WATERHEAD HOTEL in the 1920s, by Matthews of Bradford, shows a Road Traffic Act road sign but no traffic other than a girl on a cycle. The original Waterhead Hotel, built by John Stringer in 1840, is on the left with the large 1886 extension on the right.

LAKE ROAD, AMBLESIDE in the early 1920s, by Atkinson and Pollitt of Kendal, shows Mason's Art Gallery advertising an exhibition of watercolours and 'finest cruises by motor launch', with T.B. Atkinson advertising cloaks, hosiery and ladies' pyjamas. Across the road, with its motor traffic, is the sign for Robinson's 'Grocers, Provisions and Refreshments'.

FURTHER ALONG LAKE ROAD about 1910 there can be seen Marmaduke Mashiter's 'Grocers and Provisions' and Slater's Private Hotel run by Miss Agnes Slater. The photograph is by Abrahams of Keswick.

AMBLESIDE HOCKEY TEAM 1905/06, with a member on the left of the back row looking as though he has been hit on the head. On 5 October 1905 this team, playing without G. Redmayne, E. Bousefield and E. Jackson (reported to be three first class players), defeated Kendal on the Borrans field 4–0. Dr Johnston (from the Augustus Johnston and Son practice at Gale House) is reported to have defended the Ambleside goal well. All comers were apparently played for on 19 October the Ambleside Golf Club lost 6–4 to the Hockey team.

THE HOME GUARD OF THE AMBLESIDE AREA gather at Ambleside for an event with prizes during the Second World War.

THE HOSPITAL PARADE on 6 July 1913 ended with the crowning of the Rose Queen, Doris Backhouse, in Rothay Park by Mrs Storey of Loughrigg Brow. Kitty Elliott, Winnie Grisedale, Doris Clark and Elsie Barrow were Queen's attendants. Behind the Queen can be seen train bearers Eric Tyson and Jack Jackson. Organized by Mr W. Stalker, the children were trained by Miss Roberts of the Girls' School and Miss Routledge of the Infants' School. A sum of £100 was raised for the Westmorland County Hospital. (see also p. 100.)

THE WHITE LION HOTEL, AMBLESIDE. A Rigg's coach is picking up at the hotel (their coaching office was just round the corner) and at Enoch Lamb's Royal Oak Hotel. Dawson Gill's jewellers shop sign can also be seen. There were four 'famous' coach trips from Ambleside: 1. the Langdale round; 2. Coniston; 3. Keswick, and 4. Patterdale, 'none of which should be missed'.

THOMAS TAYLOR'S SALUTATION HOTEL about 1902, with the charabanc of the Prince of Wales Hotel, Grasmere, with guests, on a tour of the area. Tariff at the Salutation at the time was: Bedroom 2s.–5s.; Private sitting room 3s. 6d.–7s 6d.; Breakfast 2s.; Lunch 2s.; Tea 1s. 6d.; Dinner 3s. 6d.–5s.

STOCKGHYLL FORCE, AMBLESIDE was a highlight of a visit to Ambleside. Here the waterfalls are photographed by Brockbank of Windermere about 1910. Bulmer's Guide says: 'A pretty little waterfall in a romantic glen. The water is precipitated from a height of 70 feet in three leaps and though the liquid mass is but small the "Force" and its surroundings have engaged the pencils of artists innumerable.' The entrance fee was 3d.

THE HOSPITAL PARADE of 6 July 1913 included the schoolchildren demonstrating various local games. This shows the Maypole and 'Pitchin' groups passing Rigg's coaching and parcel receiving office in Market Place. (See p. 97).

ST ANNE'S HOME OF THE CHURCH OF ENGLAND WAIFS AND STRAYS SOCIETY at Eller Rigg, Ambleside supported twenty girls of which fourteen can be seen here.

AMBLESIDE MARKET PLACE COACHING TRAFFIC in the late nineteenth century, caught by Herbert Bell of Ambleside. Charabancs for Langdale, Coniston, Keswick and Patterdale – the four 'famous' trips – and coaches to Windermere, provided by Browns, Riggs and Taylors, were the holiday scene for many decades.

CHURCH STREET, AMBLESIDE about 1907. The shop of T. Hesmondhalgh, coal merchant, can be seen on the right of the picture.

'A QUAINT CORNER OF DEAR OLD AMBLESIDE', reads the message written on the back of the postcard. These seventeenth-century buildings at How Head in the Chapel Hill area, opposite St Anne's church, caught the attention of both artists and photographers for many years.

AMBLESIDE MARKET CROSS and the carriage stand which led to the building of a bus station in later years in a photograph of about 1905. Mrs Squires, Fancy Bazaar, Longmire and Co., Grocers, T. & A. Mackereth, Drapers and Outfitters, and H.W. Herd, Chemists, all had shops in Central Buildings on the right.

RYDAL ROAD, AMBLESIDE when it was possible to stand in the middle of the road in complete safety photographed by James Banks of Lake Road, Ambleside.

'THE WORKERS' AT AMBLESIDE SPORTS at the turn of the century include the volunteer St John Ambulance man seated in the centre of the middle row of the first picture. In the lower photograph a competitor seems to have been overdoing it and is receiving attention from three St John Ambulance men.

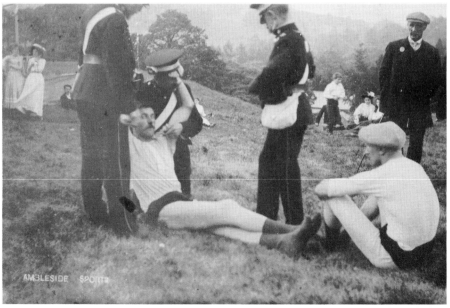

HAYTIME, WITH REPAIRS TO THE MACHINE, is here caught about 1905 by Walmsley Brothers of Ambleside. Charles and James Walmsley worked out of their studio in Rydal Road and reproduced many photographs by photogravure, such as this one, to produce cheap postcards for sale.

THE SCROGGS, LOUGHRIGG, with an advertisement for teas displayed on the garden fence in this view of about 1910. If there were a few shillings to be made from the visitors the cottagers took the opportunity.

'ON THE BRATHAY', a view of the River Brathay about 1905 as it passes the gardens of the mansion Croft. This house was occupied by Mrs Helen Cunliffe who lost her husband, Robert Ellis Cunliffe, when he died in 1902 at 54 years of age. Her only son, Thomas Henry Withers Cunliffe, 19 when the photograph was taken, was to become a Captain in the Lancashire Fusiliers and was killed at Gallipoli in 1915 aged 29.

AMBLESIDE GOLF CLUB HOUSE early in the century, by C.G. Mason, photographer of Lake Road, Ambleside. Situated near Deer Hows above Fox How and Loughrigg Brow, the Loughrigg Links were described in a guide book as 'a splendid 9-hole course, well drained and surrounded by the most magnificent scenery, within easy reach of the town'. Green fees were 2s. 6d. a day, 10s. a week, and 20s. a month.

HAYMAKING IN LOUGHRIGG about 1905, pictured by the Pictorial Stationery Co. of London in their 'Peacock' series of postcards.

THE STEPPING STONES AT AMBLESIDE were pictured by many photographers before the First World War, but here the magic of the place is caught by the Hart Publishing Co. of London who produced some of the most delightful Lake District photographs about that time. The lower picture, of Wordsworth's wishing gate on the old road from Rydal to Grasmere, is another in the series. 'Smile if thou wilt but not in scorn', said the poet.

'THE YOUNG ANGLERS, RYDAL' is the title of this charming Hart Publishing Co. picture which includes the same two young girls (were they the photographer's daughters?) as on p. 108.

NAB COTTAGE, RYDAL when the main road ran just outside the front door and the farm was run by Jonathan Armstrong. This house has many famous literary connections, in particular with De Quincy and Coleridge.

HE MAIN ROAD THROUGH RYDAL about 1902, with the lane to Rydal church and Hall on the right. 'Were we anxious, in the limits of a single day's excursion, to give a stranger the best possible conception of the beauty of the country, this road would be the last which we would choose,' says Pearson's guide. Other routes offered 'escape from the dusty high road'.

TOURISTS BY THE WAGONETTE-LOAD at Rydal about 1905. It was not unusual to have a photographer take pictures of your exciting trip, and here 'HHH' is the photographer. Presumably the party brought him with them. The first charabanc has stopped where the photographer for the last picture stood.

SKATING ON RYDAL LAKE about 1910. This postcard, sent from Southport in February 1912, carries a request to Dr Mitchell of Rothay Garth to attend. 'I have been poorly since I came here. The place upsets me very much. I have been miserable and want to go home at once. I do not like the nurses and since I cut my head they have been dreadful with me.'

WHITE MOSS COMMON, looking down from the old road at Grasmere in the 1920s, by Atkinson and Pollitt of Kendal. Dr Arnold is quoted as calling the three roads at this point 'The Radical Reform' (the then new road to Grasmere at lake level), 'The Moderate Reform' (the road over the bank by the wishing gate), and 'Old Corruption' (the older track higher up the fell).

65. COACHES DESCENDING RED BANK GRASMERE
(ABRAHAMS' SERIES)

CHARABANCS DESCENDING RED BANK, GRASMERE about 1905 by G.P. Abraham of Keswick. Most visitors were expected to walk both up and down the steeper hills and there was a long standing joke about paying so much to walk so far. When a photo was to be taken the intrepid travellers usually climbed back on board but got off again for the journey. Abrahams, who faked many Lakeland pictures, got this one right, even if they tilted the camera slightly to enhance the hill.

GRASMERE LAKE FROM RED BANK by the Hart Publishing Co. In the background is Dunmail Raise, the then boundary with the county of Cumberland. 'The incomparable beauties of Red Bank' drew walkers, cyclists and charabanc trippers every season.

THE PRINCE OF WALES HOTEL, GRASMERE photographed by Bell of Lake Road, Ambleside. Much of Herbert Bell's magnificent photography is now in archives at the Armitt Library at Ambleside and the Abbot Hall Museum of Lakeland Life at Kendal. The full story of this most remarkable of Lakeland photographers has yet to be written.

THE BACK OF DOVE COTTAGE, GRASMERE. The William Wordsworth house in Grasmere was usually pictured from the front, but this view must have satisfied the never-ending quest of Edwardian postcard collectors for something different.

DALE LODGE HOTEL, GRASMERE pictured by Brunskill of Windermere about 1902, with two charabancs and a private carriage posing for the camera. At the turn of the century Dale Lodge was run by the Elleray family as a private hotel.

THE SWAN HOTEL AT GRASMERE pictured by Pettitts of Keswick in the 1930s, with the County Council steam roller EC3930 parked in the small roadside depot that was situated there for many years.

READ'S BOOKSHOP IN GRASMERE about 1902, photographed by Brittain and Wright of Stockton in their 'Phoenix' series. Sam Read's bookshop has been very much a part of Grasmere for many years. William Baldry, the famous photographer, ran another stationers shop in Red Lion Square.

MRS E.H. BALDRY'S MOSS GROVE PRIVATE HOTEL, Grasmere photographed about 1904, un-doubtedly for the hotel's use. The sign behind the horse indicated this was a 'temperance' hotel.

'BOOK HERE FOR THE ROYAL MAIL AND LAKE DISTRICT COACHES', and 'London and North Western Railway Receiving Office' say the notices outside the Rigg's Coach Office, Grasmere, when it was photographed about 1902 by Brunskill of Windermere. The hotel bus awaits the passing Rigg's Royal Mail coach on the Windermere to Keswick run. On the left, with shutters up, is Bell's of Ambleside, chemists shop.

TWO VIEWS OF TEA GARDENS. 'Grasmere Tea Gardens' is the title of the Fothergill of Grasmere photograph of 1905 when a more formal attitude to dress is obvious. In the background is Grasmere parish church of St Oswald. In the second picture, taken from the bridge in the 1930s, a more casual style is apparent.

GRASMERE POST OFFICE with, opposite, Dodgson's bootmakers shop, run by Miles Dixon, where 'repairs were a speciality'. Abrahams of Keswick took this turn of the century view. The post office was run by Joseph Casson Hodgson, with letters arriving at 6 a.m. and 3.45 p.m. and despatched at 7.30 a.m. 10 a.m. and 7.00 p.m. 'via Windermere'.

A RIGG'S CHARABANC calls at the Grasmere Temperance Hotel about 1905 when the proprietor was Isaac Williams. He was also manager for the Elterwater Green Slate Co. Ltd.

THE GRASMERE RUSHBEARING PARADE about 1912. Six girls in green and white tunics hold the ceremonial linen sheet which was spun locally in 1891. The parade to St Oswald's church is on the nearest Sunday to the saint's day on 5 August. The church floor no longer needs a rush mat but the ceremony continues, as much a part of Grasmere as William Wordsworth and gingerbread.

GRASMERE SPORTS in the field by the New Hall about 1912. The Belsfield Hotel bus from Windermere and Taylor's coach, of the Salutation Hotel, Ambleside, can be seen among others making up a viewing stand in the foreground.

THE BAND of the 4th Battalion East Lancashire Regiment with Lt S.B. Norwood as conductor entertained the crowds at the Grasmere Sports in 1906 and for a number of years after. Previously, the Manchester Military Band (1905) and the Black Dyke Band (1904) had played. The photograph is by Lovell Mason who succeeded William Baldry as official photographer to the sports.

WRESTLERS GEORGE STEADMAN AND GEORGE LOWDON fight at the 1888 sports, as pictured by William Baldry who, a guide stated, was 'photographer, bookseller and stationer' and had 'a fancy repository and furnished houses to let'.

THE 'GUIDES' ready for their race in the 1876 sports, again pictured by Baldry. J. Greenop (second from the right) was winner in a record time of 16 minutes, 18 seconds. J. Dewyer (who won in 1875) was second and J.B. Brownrigg third. J. Greenop went on to win every year until 1882.

SOCIETY PERSONAGES at the 1899 sports, photographed by Mason, included Mrs Kennedy from Ulverston, Lord and Lady Cavendish from Holker, Viscount Cross from Broughton, Sir John Dunne, the Chief Constable, Captain Higgin Birket from Winster, Mrs Machell from Penny Bridge, and Captain A.B. Dunlop of The Howe, the chairman of the committee.

A CHARABANC FROM THE KESWICK HOTEL is pictured by Maysons of Keswick on the summit of Dunmail Raise en route to Grasmere about 1905. The back offside wheel is chained and 'skidded' for the descent. Rooms at the Keswick Hotel could be had from 2s. 6d. per night, with breakfast another 2s. 6d.

MAYSONS REVISITED THE SAME PLACE some years later to photograph one of the early hard-tyred motor charabancs driving over the pass into Cumberland. The road is still unmade.

THE TOURISTS REST AT EASEDALE TARN, run by W. Wilson, became the subject of tourist interest and postcards were made of the 'rough refreshment hut partly formed by an enormous boulder'. A boat was for hire 'for rowing or fishing'.

Easedale Valley. Grasmere.

SHEEP IN THE EASEDALE VALLEY photographed by Smiths in their 'Suitall' series in about 1902. These were a major source of income until the tourists arrived.

SKELWITH BRIDGE BOBBIN MILL, owned by Jeremiah Coward. It was the Cowards of Skelwith Bridge who helped Albert Fleming of Neum Crag and his housekeeper Marion Twelves produce the first twelve spinning wheels, based on a wheel borrowed from the Isle of Man, for the St Martins (or Langdale) Linen Industry at Elterwater in 1883.

OUTSIDE THE SKELWITH BRIDGE HOTEL, Loughrigg, Ambleside in 1906. Mr William Fleming, the licensee, is seated beside Mr Elliott, who is driving, in a trap pulled by a horse called Tommy. Weekly 'pension' then was 7s. each for a small party and 6s. for a large party. Parties of less than six were 21s. per week extra, if a private sitting room was required, says Pearson's guide of the time.

SKELWITH BRIDGE was the border of Westmorland with the county of Lancashire. Ambleside parish included the village on the Westmorland side. Photographer J. Sawyers of Kendal took his wife and one of his daughters along to provide human interest in this view of about 1902.

ST MARTINS AT ELTERWATER was the home of the Ruskin Linen Industry which, from the late nineteenth century, was part of the way of life for many of the local farms and homes, as the women of the house made linen from flax having learnt the old art of spinning with a wheel and the skills of lacemaking. Mrs Heskett (see p. 2) and her daughter Mrs Pepper were at the centre of this industry, and were left at St Martins by Canon Rawnsley when he and Miss Twelves moved to Keswick.

THE POST OFFICE AT ELTERWATER in the 1920s, pictured by Atkinson and Pollitt of Kendal. The two open tourer motor cars carry the registrations EC4197 and EC5524. The sub-postmistress was listed as Miss Mary Thackeray, but had become Mrs Mary Holmes by 1929.

PLANTING THE MAPLE TREE at Elterwater Green for the Jubilee of King George V. The *Westmorland Gazette* of 15 May 1937 carried a picture of Joseph Gaskell, who had planted the tree, sitting on a memorial seat placed nearby for the coronation in 1937 of King George VI. Joseph was shown looking at the sapling he had planted the year before. In the foreground of this picture, watching Joseph Gaskell, is Fleming Mawson, the local grocer. The tree gave the name Maple Tree Corner to this part of the village.

THE BRITANNIA INN at the turn of the century, when John Dixon held the licence. Very much a working village then, this was the 'local', rather than a holiday inn.

ELTERWATER GREEN in the late 1920s, by Atkinson and Pollitt of Kendal. The maple tree has yet to arrive.

ELTERWATER GUNPOWDER WORKS HORSES on their annual May Day parade on 1 May 1907. These horses took the gunpowder to Windermere railway station, the gunpowder carriages being spaced twenty minutes apart in case of accident.

GUNPOWDER WORKERS pose with their product in the late nineteenth century in this photograph by M. Davies of Queen St, Millom. The boxes carry the legend 'Extra Special – Compressed', and three sticks can be seen on the top box. The works, opened in 1824, was run originally by the Huddlestone family but became part of the Nobel Group in 1918 and, later, ICI.

A SLEEPING CABIN on the Langdale Estate pictured by Atkinson and Pollitt in the early 1930s. The site would have been a hut used for either mixing or storing gunpowder until the gunpowder works closed in 1930. The transformation of the defunct gunpowder works into a holiday village in the middle of the 1930s depression was a stroke of genius as many other local explosive works sites fell into disuse. The postcard dated 1940 carries the message: 'Having a great time here. This is our cabin, there are six altogether in it.'

THE ENTRANCE TO THE LANGDALE ESTATE in the 1930s, by Atkinson and Pollitt, shows the transformation from gunpowder works, complete with reception, café and a 'here you are' sign. The *Westmorland Gazette* of 6 March 1936 said, 'If Langdale hasn't exactly turned swords into ploughshares it has at any rate turned its gunpowder works into a great Paradise. It is a paradise open to all descendants of Adam and Eve on holiday bent.'

INSIDE THE GATEWAY CAFE RESTAURANT in the 1930s by Atkinson and Pollitt. Note the handmade chairs and tables. 'None go away without registering an inner vow to come again at the first opportunity,' said the advertising of the time.

THE WHITE LION HOTEL, CHAPEL STILE, with the postman at the door, in about 1902 when John Bowness held the licence. The Bowness family were at the White Lion for decades as well as being the local blacksmith and grocer. The photograph is by Atkinsons of Ulverston.

GREAT LANGDALE SCHOOL about 1905 when Thomas Fisher was the schoolmaster. The school was built in 1824 by the Elterwater Gunpowder Company and was long the school for the children of the quarry and gunpowder workers.

TWO VIEWS OF CHAPEL STILE. In the first, of the 1920s by Atkinson and Pollitt, the view is from the main road through the valley, and in the second, by Atkinson of Ulverston from about 1902, a closer view of the Holy Trinity church at the foot of Silverhow is given.

INSIDE LANGDALE CHURCH in the 1920s when the lighting was still by oil lamp but central heating had been installed. The church was built in 1857 for the cost of £1,600 given entirely by Mr J. Robinson and Mr E.B. Wheatley. The nave was extended in 1880. Photograph by Atkinson and Pollitt of Kendal.

'VIEW UP LANGDALE VALLEY' was the title of this 1920s view by Atkinson and Pollitt. The unmade road and lack of traffic illustrate how much times have changed.

AN EARLIER VIEW nearer to the end of the valley shows the Pikes with the plantation below which was lost at the time of the First World War. The bridge over the beck in Great Langdale with the view of the Stickle Ghyll appeared on many Edwardian postcards. How many people realise that the tarn above was a water supply for the gunpowder works?

THE DUNGEON GHYLL HOTEL with a charabanc coach at the door about 1904 when Joseph Youdell was the licensee for both the old and new hotels. The four in hand coaches took visitors over by Blea Tarn into Little Langdale or to Grasmere over Red Bank. The hotel was the lunch break on the Little Langdale – Great Langdale – Grasmere – Rydal 'round tour' from Ambleside.

WALLEND HOLIDAY CAMP, Great Langdale pictured by G.P. Abraham of Keswick. Behind is the unmade road to Blea Tarn and Little Langdale. What would the 'planners' say today?

A RIGG'S CHARABANC COACH on the Langdale round trip about 1905, again by Abrahams of Keswick. The unmade road from Blea Tarn into Great Langdale must have provided an exciting experience as the horses pulled the chained and 'skidded' coach downhill, digging deep ruts in the road surface in doing so.

THE THRANG QUARRY at Chapel Stile was worked alongside the larger Elterwater Quarry. Raphael Tuck recorded the working of the quarry for posterity with a series of postcards. In this picture face workers clear the working face by using ropes.

SPLITTERS WORKING SLATE at Thrang Quarry in another of the Raphael Tuck series. What made amusing postcards for the visitor was dirty, often cold and wet work for poor wages for the local quarrymen.

MIDDLEFELL FARM, GREAT LANGDALE at the turn of the century, when Jeremiah Grisedale and his family ran the farm and provided apartments and meals for visitors.

LOW COLWITH FARM, LITTLE LANGDALE with Mr and Mrs John Greenhow and son Jonathan, about 1910. The famous Colwith Falls are on the lands of High Colwith farm, then occupied by the Wren family. Thomas Wren ran a 'refreshments room' in the season. 'The key for Colwith Force is obtainable at the cottage immediately over the bridge,' says Pearson's guide. 'The charge is threepence.'

THE TOURIST'S REST, Little Langdale about 1902 by Atkinson of Ulverston, when William Parry was the 'licensed victualler'. This is now the Three Shires Inn.

GEORGE KIRKBY BOWNESS AND FAMILY from New Houses, Little Langdale about 1906. George was the blacksmith at the quarry, had his own smallholding, and ran a wagonette for hire. With him are his wife Annie (née Atkinson) and children (back row) Agnes and Henry, (middle row) Annie Mary, Fred (between his parents), Dora and John, and (front row) Thomas and William.

ELIZABETH YOUDELL OF HIGH BIRK HOW, Little Langdale with pet lambs in the late nineteenth century. Elizabeth married at 32 years of age and, as Mrs Hodgson, mothered eight children. This photograph is from the family album of the Hodgsons of Wilson Place, Little Langdale. (See also p. 142.)

HAYMAKING IN FORGE FIELD (at the end of Greenbank Terrace) in the 1950s with, left to right: John Birkett, Ted Nevinson, Jim Hodgson and George Birkett. A way of life – farming with horses and using carts for collecting the hay – was fast coming to a close.

THE ESKDALE AND ENNERDALE FOXHOUNDS included the Langdales in their area. They are seen here in the yard at the Tourist's Rest in the late 1920s with Bob Simmonds and his daughters Freda and Kathleen, Teddy Foster, Peter Hodgson of Birk How, William Porter (the huntsman), and William Dixon (the licensee). The constant fight against the fox was turning into a 'sporting' pastime, the reason for its continuance being the carnage caused by foxes raiding farms and fields.

BESSY (ELIZABETH) HODGSON taking tea to Peter Hodgson in the hay field behind Little Langdale school on Birk How farm about 1944.

SHEEP SHEARING at Fell Foot, Little Langdale when Elijah Mutton was the farmer. The picture, by Atkinsons of Ulverston about 1902, includes Mrs Mutton and their son George. The farm at Fell Foot had previously been occupied by the Tysons and was to be farmed by the Youdells in the 1920s. It is famous for its connection with Lanty Slee, the smuggler of illicit liquor.

INSIDE LITTLE LANGDALE SCHOOL about 1900, when Mrs Emma Wade, schoolmistress, lived at the school house with Mrs Mary Pepper. Little Langdale School was built in 1865 and was also used for church services. Pupils were taken from the northern reaches of Lancashire, children such as the Nelsons walking over from Tilberthwaite each day whatever the weather.

THE PUPILS OF THE SCHOOL with the three members of staff in the same era. Many of these children walked many miles over very hilly country to get to school and return home each day. School diaries, which all Westmorland schools kept, show that on many occasions in winter pupils were just not able to get to the school.

TWO RATHER SPECIAL PHOTOGRAPHS taken just after the First World War of two families who attended Little Langdale School. The top picture shows Abigail Nelson and her brother Robin from Holme Ground, Tilberthwaite (their mother was Abigail Pepper from St Martins Ruskin Linen Industry), and the lower picture, Jim, Mary and Peter Hodgson of Ash Lea, Little Langdale. The two boys were in their sailor suits for the day the photographer called.

IN THE SUMMER of 1941 photographer N.A. Scurrah of Stanningley near Leeds stayed at Birk How farm, Little Langdale on holiday, and at Christmas that year the family received this picture of Peter Hodgson at the porch gate. Farming and quarrying had been his life in spite of a good school record.

FELL FOOT FARM AND THE BLEA TARN PASS into Great Langdale with the Pikes behind are all in the picture of about 1902 by Atkinson of Ulverston. This is also the road over the Wrynose Pass to the West, the furthest point west of Westmorland.

SHEEP COLLECTING ON WRYNOSE PASS during the Second World War, from the Hodgson family album at Wilson Place, Little Langdale. This was a Roman route through the Lakeland passes to the west coast and has connected the locals of Langdale with the families in Dunnerdale and Eskdale over the centuries since. The road remained unmade until after the war.

THE THREE SHIRE STONE mentioned only Lancashire but was sited at a point where the counties of Lancashire, Westmorland and Cumberland met on the summit of the Wrynose Pass. This picture by Atkinson and Pollitt is of about 1930.

Kirkstone Pass to Ullswater

KIRKSTONE PASS in the late 1920s as seen by Maysons of Keswick, with a Daimler motor charabanc climbing the pass from the Ullswater side. Improved motor transport was opening the Lake District to round trips by motor coach from the Lancashire and north-east industrial towns and a traffic problem was developing that lasts until today.

RIGG'S ULLSWATER COACH leaving Ambleside about 1905, pictured by Abrahams of Keswick as the climb up 'the struggle' onto Kirkstone Pass is started. The usual four in hand are assisted by two extra horses with an outrider.

KIRKSTONE PASS INN is the background for this 1911 Coronation Day outing to the Lake District by motor charabanc. The days of the horse charabanc were nearly at an end.

THE BROTHERSWATER HOTEL, with two Rigg's coaches carrying the Kendal Zion Chapel choir and friends on an outing to Ullswater on 5 August 1907. 'Just to make you smile' was the message on the back of the postcard.

THE MILLCRESTS HOTEL, GLENRIDDING with a Rigg's coach and an open tourer motor car about 1910, by Abrahams of Keswick. Many postcards are for sale at the tourist shops opposite the hotel.

KILNER'S TEA GARDEN, PATTERDALE in the late 1920s, by Atkinson and Pollitt of Kendal. For many decades William Kilner had run an apartments business from Rose Cottage, with Thomas and Margaret Kilner later taking over the Grisedale Bridge 'apartments' trade.

ST PATRICK'S HOLY WELL at the roadside at the head of Ullswater is said to be associated with the saint who baptised early Christians there. Unlike other holy wells in the district this one survived the centuries and is complete with a Victorian canopy. Seen here is a Rigg's coach passing the well about 1905.

THE ULLSWATER FOXHOUNDS on their meet of 30 March 1907 – 'for Place Fell'. The huntsman was Joe Bowman and the terriers coupled together were Turk and Trimmer. The Eskdale, the Ullswater, and the Blencathra were names given to packs of fox hounds which, with others, provided coverage of most of the Lakeland Fells working an annual routine understood by all the farming community.

THE PENRITH BOY SCOUTS pose for their photograph at Patterdale on Good Friday 1911. The Scout movement was then only six years old and it is interesting to see the original uniform. The First World War was only three years away.

THE ULLSWATER HOTEL is the background for the Riggs coach in this turn of the century view by Stengel. The Bownass family had the Ullswater Hotel for many decades and offered posting and boating as added facilities. Rooms were 2s. 6d.–6s. (single 5s.); 'pension' 63s.–70s. per week; breakfast 1s. 6d.–2s. 6d., lunch 2s. 6d.–3s. and dinner 4s.

THE PATTERDALE PIER was at the end of the Ullswater Hotel garden for many years, and here the steamer *Raven* (built 1889) is pictured by Valentine of Dundee. Converted to diesel in 1934, the *Raven* is still at work on the lake.

THE POOLEY BRIDGE PIER was in the county of Cumberland, the River Eamont being the boundary. In this 1930s view both the rebuilt *Raven* and the *Lady of the Lake* can be seen.

POOLEY BRIDGE is at an ancient crossing point of the River Eamont at the eastern end of Ullswater. It stands in the ancient parish of Barton under the shadow of Dunmallet hill fort. The village had a market for cattle, sheep and fish. This postcard, posted May 1906, carries the message, 'It is Miss Kirk in the chair.'

THE POOLEY BRIDGE FOOTBALL TEAM just before the First World War. Reports of matches in various leagues between village teams in both the Association and the Rugby Union game can be read in the local papers of the time.

INSIDE BARTON CHURCH OF ST MICHAEL when the lighting was by oil lamp but after the 1903 restoration which renewed the seating. The great age of the church is attested by the early arch.

THE CROWN AND MITRE AT BAMPTON with a number of carriages posed for Reed of Penrith, George Clark was the licensed victualler 'and farmer' at the time. The postcard, posted in May 1906, describes visiting Penrith market where '20,000 eggs were for sale at 15 for a shilling and new butter is 11 pence per pound'.

THE POST OFFICE AT BAMPTON was run by Miss Ada Bell Corless when this view of 1904 was taken by Reeds of Penrith. 'Letters arrive 7.55 a.m. and are despatched at 3.35 p.m. via Penrith, and arrive 8.10 a.m. and are despatched 4.35 p.m. in summer and 3.35 p.m. in winter via Shap. No Sunday business,' said a guide. Other views of the district around the River Eamont are included in *The Eden Valley in Old Photographs*.

SWINDALE CHAPEL was a remote outpost of the vicar of Shap. Erected in 1749, with seating for 68 and a school attached to the west end, the church was repaired in 1855 and 1875 to be closed by Manchester Corporation Water Department in the 1930s. This postcard was sent to Miss Forster of Bampton from Sarah Greenhow of Truss Gap, Swindale, 'Happy New Year 31 December 1909'

THE DUN BULL HOTEL, MARDALE on a postcard posted in 1905 when Harry Usher was victualler and farmer. The tennis court, the old inn with its Victorian extension and the farm buildings at the rear can all be seen. The Haweswater Act of 1919 spelled the end for this hostelry and its community.

THE INN seen from the road that came across the valley from the church only a few years later. Work to dam the valley started in 1930 and continued throughout that decade.

'MARDALE CHURCH occupies a picturesque situation by the road side, embosomed among trees which almost conceal the diminutive edifice from view,' read a guide of 1905. It was claimed the church would hold fifty persons.

INSIDE THE CHURCH OF THE HOLY TRINITY, Mardale with the words 'Let All Thy Works Praise Thee' over the east window. Parts of the interior were reused by the Diocese of Carlisle and some of the stonework went into the reservoir draw off tower. The church was too small to accommodate the crowds that turned up for the last service on 18 August 1935 when loudspeakers conveyed the service to the crowds in surrounding fields. Demolition took place in 1936.

THE DUN BULL was the venue for the annual shepherds' meet, when lost sheep were swopped, much news passed on, and a good time was had by all. This is the 1908 meet with about eighty-five people in the picture and just over fifty sheep. The meet moved to Bampton in 1936 as the valley was being flooded.

HAWESWATER before the Manchester Corporation dam raised the water level by nearly 100 ft. The road in those days ran via Measand, where the school was situated, on the west side of the valley.

ISAAC COOKSON photographed at Bampton by J. Hardman who, in photographs, raised this Mardale shepherd to a fame he would not have believed possible. He attended Mardale shepherds' meet sixty-four times and, with others, resented the removal to Bampton. He was a man of the fells who must now stand for the spirit of the lost community of Mardale.

ACKNOWLEDGEMENTS

The production of this book would not have been possible without the assistance, in various ways, of the following south Cumbria folk:

Mrs Jean Marsh
Victoria Slowe and Janet Dugdale of Abbot Hall, who encouraged the start of the project
Christine Strickland and Sylvia Mallinson of the Kendal Library Local Studies Collection
Mrs E. Baker (née Woof), late of Kendal
Mrs Beattie of Kendal for the Grasmere Sports material
Mr George Dawson for use of the N. Carradice photographic collection
Percy and Margaret Duff of Kendal
Mrs K. Hayhurst of Burton
Mrs Hodgson of Wilson Place, Little Langdale
Mr N. Honeyman of Barrow-in-Furness
Mrs L. Knowles (née Huck) of Selside
Mr T.W. Moss of Kendal and Mr C.H. Moss of Troutbeck Bridge
Mr and Mrs F. Nevinson of Langdale, Selside and Kendal
Mrs A. Reed of Kendal
Miss O. Wilson, formerly of Rigmaden
Those people of the area into whose families this book intrudes, and the many others who encourage and support me in the collection of local old photographic images.